Don Watson is the author of many books, including *Recollections of a Bleeding Heart*, *Death Sentence*, *Watson's Dictionary of Weasel Words*, *Caledonia Australis*, *American Journeys*, *The Bush* and most recently *There It Is Again*.

Little Books on Big Themes

Fleur Anderson *On Sleep*

Katharine Murphy *On Disruption*

Sarah Ferguson *On Mother*

Nikki Gemmell *On Quiet*

Blanche d'Alpuget *On Lust & Longing*

Leigh Sales *On Doubt*

Germaine Greer *On Rage*

Barrie Kosky *On Ecstasy*

David Malouf *On Experience*

Malcolm Knox *On Obsession*

Gay Bilson *On Digestion*

Anne Summers *On Luck*

Robert Dessaix *On Humbug*

Julian Burnside *On Privilege*

Elisabeth Wynhausen *On Resilience*

Susan Johnson *On Beauty*

Don Watson

On Indignation

MELBOURNE
UNIVERSITY
PRESS

MELBOURNE UNIVERSITY PRESS
An imprint of Melbourne University Publishing Limited
Level 1, 715 Swanston Street, Carlton, Victoria 3053, Australia
mup-contact@unimelb.edu.au
www.mup.com.au

First published 2008
Text © Don Watson, 2008, 2018
This edition published 2018
Design and typography © Melbourne University Publishing Limited,
2008, 2018

Every attempt has been made to locate the copyright holders for material
quoted in this book. Any person or organisation that may have been
overlooked or misattributed may contact the publisher.

Text design by Alice Graphics
Cover design by Nada Backovic Design
Author photograph by Susan Gordon Brown
Typeset by Typeskill
Printed in Australia by McPherson's Printing Group

A catalogue record for this
book is available from the
National Library of Australia

9780522873771 (paperback)
9780522873788 (ebook)

It begins with the tease at the heart of existence. We are solipsists by nature: the world, as the philosopher said, is my world. But there's a catch. Only the part of the world that I can understand is my world, and even then it's mine only so far as I can express my understanding. The limits of my language are the limits of my world. Thus existence asserts my sublime personal dominion and my insect-like irrelevance at the same time. The Lord gives and the Lord takes away. Why—unless I am sedated or naturally insensible—would I not be indignant? And God saw that it was good? Good for Him maybe.

But not good enough. Never good enough. Whatever else we may lack in comparison, when we are indignant we may be likened to our Maker. 'Behold, the name of the LORD cometh from far, burning with His anger, and the burden thereof is heavy: His lips are full of indignation, and His tongue is a devouring fire.' Long before the Lord cometh to Isaiah He came upon Adam and Eve: and what was His judgement on their original sin if not the original fit of righteous indignation? And what also if not a fantastically egotistical self-indulgence and a model for every tyrant since?

The Lord's pride was hurt. He felt His children's dalliance as an attack on His Self. Today we would cry out: 'This is not about *You*!'

Our history is alleged to begin with a bout of indignation, and according to the prophets and the Book of Revelation it will end in the same way: in the 'day of indignation', as the King James Version and American evangelicals put it. 'Behold, I shall make thee know what shall be in the last end of the indignation: for at the time appointed the end shall be.'

Indignation is the ground bass of the Old Testament: God's indignation, the indignation of the wicked and the indignation of the good, the indignation of God's people on His behalf and on their own. Revelation says sinners shall drink at 'the cup of His indignation', which is to say, one presumes, they will drink fire and brimstone. In Deuteronomy, Yahweh warns His chosen people that if they do not obey Him He will inflict upon them every imaginable cruelty: and indeed He did and 'rooted them out of their land in anger, and in wrath, and in great indignation'. God's indignation is never much less than fatal or excruciating; it is often fiery, sometimes cleansing and invariably terrible. When God pours out His indignation it is like a nuclear blast, and in the Book of Daniel and elsewhere it is terminal. Sometimes it rains on only those guilty of abominations and the good find shelter from the blast. Just as often God is merciless to the abominable and the pure alike. The Old Testament God did not practise mindfulness. His omniscience did not make him cool.

If in general less deadly than God's, the indignation of His people can be no less consequential. Hagar mocks Sarah, or so Sarah thinks, and Sarah is indignant. She demands Abraham send Hagar away. So Abraham banishes Hagar and Ishmael, her son—and from Ishmael's line come the Arabs and the Prophet Mohammed. Noah drinks too much wine and falls asleep uncovered. Ham mocks his father's nakedness and Noah is indignant. He banishes Ham—and from Ham's posterity Africa is populated. The Bible tells us that indignation was the saltpetre of early human civilisation, that from domestic spats and cruelties the human world was shaped. Whenever someone gets his back up, calamity looms on the plain. '[W]hen Haman saw Mordecai in the king's gate, that he stood not up, nor moved for him, he was full of indignation against Mordecai.' And the Book of Esther goes on to tell how in his indignation Haman determined to kill all the Jews in Persia.

The trick, the Old Testament is always telling us, is not to cause offence to God. A few manage to do this, but more don't and the reasons for their failure are not always clear. There is no reasoning with Him, as Job learns: 'thou … increasest thine indignation upon me; changes and war are upon me', but he is a long while waiting for an explanation. We may be indignant on God's behalf, but never on our own: to be indignant on our own behalf, or even on behalf of loved ones recently murdered at His direction, is to be indignant against *Him*. 'Curse God and die!' Dictators echo the sentiment, as they do the random lethality.

God (or the tyrant) being first in everything fundamental, it is in His mind that indignation's primary rhetoric is formed: 'How dare you!' How dare you presume to know His will; or go into Egypt without asking; or complain when your whole family is slaughtered! Do not earn *His* wrath, by questioning *His* judgement, breaking *His* rules, belittling *Him*, worshipping other Gods before *Him*. Only *He* is to be worshipped. One is to obey His commandments, the whole ten of them, seven of which begin 'Thou shalt not'. One is to live in obedience and, while somehow contriving to love Him at the same time, never cease to fear

His boundless ego and bottomless, unpredictable rage. One must do it because on one's good behaviour hangs not only the safety of the city and the tribe, but the prospect of immortality. Thus God inclines the faithful to judgements even more indignant than His own: in addition to the upright and merciful, zealots, inquisitors, spies, executioners and pedants act in His name.

And why would they not when He scarcely ever makes known His motives or intentions? Silence—seemingly permanent withdrawal—is His most awful weapon. 'Hide not thy face from thy servant', pleads the Psalmist, one of multitudes to do so in the long history of religion. 'Affection all converted into indignation: an implacable indignation; slow, equable, silent, like that of a god.' Thomas Carlyle happened to be describing Dante in Giotto's portrait, but it might have been the Judeo–Christian God whose long absences and seeming indifference to suffering made all the varieties of humanism so attractive—at least until Stalin and his 'implacable indignation … like that of a God'. It might have been Yahweh or Stalin: or it might have been one of several of my relations.

Among my family, most of them descending from the Calvinist coast of Scotland, were many who had this much in common with the tribes of the Judean wilderness: they struggled to get through a week without taking umbrage at some piddling thing and wishing the offender one way or another to damnation. They did a good deal of internalising. They practised long silences. In subtle ways this constant exercise of pride probably held the family together—at least what remained of it when the unworthy had been banished. Anthropologists long ago observed the same principle in what used to be called primitive societies. It is functional after a fashion, and often funny after the event. But it is rarely fun at the time.

By way of example, while riding the five miles that separated his half-cleared hundred acres from the nearest town, a grandfather of mine convinced himself that a Mrs H had just slighted him outside the general store. He already suspected the woman of flattering herself that the few sheep she and her husband ran put them in a rank above people like him who milked cows. Construing something 'superior' in her expression when he had raised his hat to her that afternoon, very soon after he was at the mercy of his pride. As he rode home, the poison thickened in his blood, and by the time he got inside his house it had gripped him like a python. It is 'a highly characteristic sign' of indignation, Charles Darwin wrote, when 'the wings of the nostrils are somewhat raised to allow of a free indraught of air'. No sooner had my grandfather sat down for a cup of tea, than his nostrils flared like a Jersey bull's and with a great indraught of air, he slapped his hat back on his head and, telling his sons to get on with the milking, fairly flew out the door. For the boys watching from the porch that

late afternoon, the sight of their father flash-
ing between the gum trees as he galloped
down the road that led back to town and the
residence of Mrs H became a permanent
memory.

He was a soldier settler not long back
from the Great War, and this was the strange
part of it: after three years enduring everything the Axis and the northern European
winter could throw at a man, including
Passchendaele, Ypres, Mouquet Farm, Mont
St Quentin and the Spanish flu, who would
have thought he could be bothered by such
a trifle? They say war changes a man, but it
does not change all of him: nothing short
of shell shock or physical brain damage will
change whatever frames the self-possession
demanded by battle. This is what survives of

him at war's end. If Ulysses had one thing left when he got home it was self-possession, along with the indignation necessary to protect it. It was indignation—with the goddess Athena's connivance—that drove him to slaughter his wife's suitors.

Indignation is tied with very taut strings to the instinct for self-preservation. It is related directly to death in the same way that humiliation is. When Athena stirs it up, she demonstrates one of the preeminent affinities of our nature: between taking personal offence and taking lives. The Old Testament makes the same point repeatedly. Samuel, for instance, appears to find hacking Philistines and sacrificial animals to pieces no impediment to getting on with life and making a success of it. It comes naturally.

Those earlier members of my family did not actually hack at each other or their neighbours, but they often had them on their minds as day after day they hacked at weeds and routed trees and no doubt remembered the words of the Psalm: 'Let their eyes be darkened, that they see not; and make their loins continually to shake. Pour out thine indignation upon them … let them be blotted out of the book of the living.' The words which are said to foretell the instruction and fate of Jesus, in fact foretell the instruction of whole tribes and nations, and the fates of millions. Psalm 69 is the psalm for the indignant; the ones trapped in the chaff-cutter of their own righteousness, whose zeal has created enemies exceeding the number of hairs on their heads, their mother's sons among them.

'O God, thou knowest my foolishness'. It could have been our family motto.

Indignation is passed on through generations as surely as red hair or haemophilia. It is also contagious. The soldier settler's sisters were even touchier than he was, and their cat caught it. It glared and spat at every other living thing, which in turn made visitors indignant. In a similar vein, Mrs H, who I imagine had felt nothing but bewilderment when my forebear confronted her among the washing on her clothesline, was very soon gripped with indignation of her own. To accuse her of slighting him—it really was too much. To think that she would bother slighting such as he! She! What did he take her for? He! What did he take himself for? Him! Her! And so on. Having caught his indignation, as it were, they fought like scorpions to a standstill and he went home silent and exhausted.

It is doubtful if he had learned anything. Indignation is not a learning environment. But the truth, had his mood allowed him to see it, was that he liked sheep. Nothing would have made him happier than to have a couple of paddocks full of Romney Marsh ewes and wethers, as Mrs H did. 'Nobody lies as much as the indignant do', Nietzsche said: and often to *themselves*, he might have added.

For people who hate nothing more than giving offence to others and have no taste for strife, the difficulty is always to know what it is that will offend. There are more or less universal insults concerning the character of one's mother, the size of one's genitals, the gait of one's horse, etc.; but those and a few others aside, there are almost as many sensitivities in the world as there are people to offend them. While some can be read in the briefest acquaintance or just by looking at a person, at least as many are hidden from the most astute beholder, if not from the person herself. And then there are some—Don Quixote, for example, and also a great aunt of mine—whose mere appearance invites obvious insults, yet to these they are immune; while a mild remark about some seemingly unconnected thing will cause them to explode and demand a duel to the death. It depends of course on what the person imagines he is or most wants to be—of what he thinks his worth consists. The facts of this may be hidden not only from the person giving offence, but from the person taking it, and the fit of pique that follows—even one that lasts for years—might never be understood or explained by either of them. These hurts are as much like allergies as psychological conditions, but unlike both those common afflictions, have no cure outside opium or religion.

As with Don Quixote, who is a very knowing madman, the person prone to fits of indignation is frequently expert at teasing fits from others. Like those parasite birds that ride on the cow's back, the tease lives off the indignant: he whispers in their ears, baits them; like Satan or Athena he plays the Id. In my own childhood someone was always trying to get a rise, and someone was always stalking off in tears and slamming doors behind her; or marching out of the cowshed and down the hill as if determined that the rest of us would never see her again. 'Huffs', they were called, or 'scots'. But the indignant very often walk into a void. They need resistance. And sooner or later they have to come in for tea. What then? What does it profit a man to throw his custard at the wall?

For the incurably indignant, one answer is silence, the complete fadeout: deep, long, infuriating, inexplicable silence. For the silent one, this is the equivalent of the prophets' sojourns in the desert. If he stays there long enough, he can imagine he has entered a higher state, perhaps even a state of grace, certainly a state beyond the reach of his own feelings that would otherwise be gnawing at his innards like so many rats. For those who have to cope with this style of protest, indignation does not begin to describe their feelings—they would happily kill them. Cain is a case in point. Jealousy—indignation at God's outrageous and, as usual, unexplained favouritism—might have driven him to murder his brother: but who ever heard that story without suspecting that Abel was a psychological martyr long before his brother whacked him and created the first real one?

I had uncles in the mould of Abel. And aunts in the mould of Cain. Uncles and great-uncles who though they shared the same roof exchanged no more than sighs for weeks on end; uncles who were cast out forever by aunts who for unfathomable reasons went lifetimes without speaking to other aunts.

It is not to deprive us of their wisdom and personal charm that they don't speak; it is to prey on our consciences. They will have us feel guilty. With silence they will grind us until we confess our wrongdoing. Hurl cow pats at me, they say; make me bleed; nail me up: I will not cry out. You will not have the satisfaction.

This kind of martyrdom is indignation's closest relation—the brother, if you like. It is both a weapon and a way of surviving the incipient civil war in families. It issues from the never-ending drama of the self, not least the self's innate capacity for fantasy, megalomania and envy. Indignation and martyrdom: those two were just about my chief inheritances.

Jesus—at least as he was taught to us—was to the Old Testament God as lithium is to hypomania. He tried to put a check on indignation, which might be one reason why He taught with parables rather than rules. The effect of the New Testament on the cosmology of my youth was irremediable confusion: chaos and hellfire and piety. One moment I was as if commanded by the inner voice to let fly in righteous anger like Samson among the Philistines or Jesus in the temple, the next retreating in the glow of the Beatitudes, murmuring, turn the other cheek, blessed are the peacemakers, blessed are the meek, suffer the little children, don't be like your grandfather.

In my eleventh and twelfth years I lived equally impressed by God's awful power and the sweet possibilities of the Sermon on the Mount. Soon enough, however, I found that while I could do without loving my enemy I could not live without bouts of indignation. There is too much pleasure in it. I was drawn as if my body needed it as much as salt and carbohydrate. The Karamazov brother might have been feeling as I did when he said that he didn't want harmony. 'From love of humanity I don't want it … I would rather remain with my unavenged suffering and unsatisfied indignation. Besides, too high a price is asked for harmony; it's beyond our means to pay so much to enter on it.' It was not just the adrenaline rush or the perverse delight in chaos, or the even purer form of pleasure that withdrawal brings: it was my inability to imagine much more than bore-dom flowing from Christian serenity. I inher-ited, or had reinforced in me, a roughly equal measure of pious obedience and indignant revolt: a loathsome amalgam, especially in a child. Not that I recognised it, but I know I always felt better when my unconscious was decent enough to push me in one direction at a time.

Indignation is anger, but not quite the same. Anger has a less specific character. We feel indignant when we're jilted, deceived, betrayed, cheated, traduced, overtaken on a double line, suffer rudeness from a bank teller, impertinence from a dental hygienist: when we've had one too many lousy rolls of the dice. We may feel it if some remote extension of our being is insulted: our children or our dog, our car or refrigerator, our God, our horse. Jockeys say that it is safer to insult a horse's owner or tell him his wife is ugly than to tell him that his horse is slow or lacks heart. Some time in the future, by using advanced infra-red photography, it might be possible to map the emotional reach of every individual in a country town or suburb—or a school or penitentiary.

The feeling often fades as quickly as it flares, but it can last for years as well. It can poison the soul. It may seem to pass and then resurface much later, possibly in an unexplained tic or catatonia. It may grow into anger or rage: into force for that matter—into violence, murder and war. Castles and battleships, cannons and grenades are, in certain lights, physical expressions of human indignation. It has roots in fear, bitterness, shyness, desire and every unsatisfied need of the flesh and the spirit. Our indignation barks inside us; bursts forth and retreats like another personality, like Dr Jekyll's Mr Hyde. It can grow into psychosis—*Psycho*'s Norman Bates burbles with childish indignation.

Anger obliterates personality. Indignation expresses it. Indignation is full of dramatic, including comic, possibility; anger is never funny and whether it is real or feigned, soon becomes uncomfortable and drab to witness. Charlie Chaplin did indignation all the time, anger only rarely. It is the same with many of the great comic turns: Katharine Hepburn, Lucille Ball, James Stewart, Stan Laurel, Tony Hancock—they were all good at indignation. It is one of possibly two emotions on which Harrison Ford has built his stellar career.

Very likely it has something to do with the spectacle of a grown-up behaving like a toddler. As a two-year-old wails when some part of his world is taken away or it behaves in ways that he cannot control, the comedian wails when his pride is punctured or deflated, when his monomania meets reality. So, sometimes, does the theatrical gangster; like Edward G Robinson when the end comes in *Little Caesar*: 'Mother of Mercy, is this the end of Rico?'

The Puritan mind was much concerned with 'training the will' of the child, beating down the stubbornness and pride it brings into the world. '*I*, when it relates to God, is expressive of His dignity … When used with reference to men, it expresses their pride', wrote an eighteenth-century Presbyterian. Nothing in human nature is more likely to oppose God's will than the individual will.

It is obvious in the two-year-old who only
knows gratification or indignation. Just as it
learns to walk and talk and exercise its will,
it encounters new threats to its control. It
must surrender omnipotence and make do
with some less satisfying notion, such as
'God is present in each one of His creatures'.
The Puritans reckoned this was the deci-
sive moment: train the child to walk God's
path, speak God's word, do God's will, or
let him will his own way to perdition. As
the unbroken will stood between every child
and submission to God's purpose, it stood,
quite literally, between heaven and hell. Mrs
Wesley was in no doubt that the success so
clearly manifest in her godly sons, John and
Charles, could be put down to her breaking their infant wills. Thereafter *righteous*

indignation was the only indignation available to them.

Pride thus comes before the greatest of all falls, the fall from grace and into the arms of the devil. In the days when Puritans were holding witch-hunts, wilfulness—including indignation of the unrighteous kind—was one of the forms of behaviour likely to get a person into trouble. Among people who fear God and value peace and harmony, the chronically wilful represent the gravest threat. That they should risk their own souls by refusing to humble themselves before God is bad enough; but their wilfulness places the whole community in peril of His wrath. In such places those not doing God's work perforce must do the Devil's. The Puritans redrew in civil society the line long drawn in

Christian religious establishments: between the righteous indignation of the Godly and the fiendish indignation of the wilful.

In an early episode of *The Sopranos*, the psychopathic Paulie Walnuts orders a coffee in what looks very like a Starbucks. Paulie's will, plainly, was not broken as a child. No self-respecting capo's was. There would be no show if their wills had been broken. An entire film genre would be lost. Paulie has never been in a Starbucks or any place like it before. He feels threatened: anything unfamiliar is a threat to Paulie Walnuts. The middle-class blonde girl taking orders for triple mocha supremes and espresso macchiatos issues from a culture as far removed from the Sicilian and the criminal as it is possible to be. The combustible Paulie looks around with his customary aggression. Everything about the place gets under his skin. We invented this stuff, he says: so how come these other people are making money from it? How come we didn't get into it? What's the matter with us? Within moments he's burning with the offence to his dignity and his family's dignity, and to what is just and proper. He puts a stove-top espresso pot inside his coat.

Honour and indignation are elements of the same environment. Money is another one. Money—the 'points'—is the one thing that will keep Paulie's mood stable. So long as he's getting his 'points' he's tolerably pacific. If he's not, only blood will console him. The relationship between money and pride is a perpetual theme of *The Sopranos*, as it is in most films about gangsters—and also in nineteenth-century novels and some of the plays of Shakespeare. It is a theme of human history, which is not surprising given that money—whatever form it takes or name it goes by—weighs the worth accorded to the person paid it. Whether it comes as ochre or diamonds, shekels or wampum or virgins, what we now call money has always been taken personally. Dollars could as well be called 'indignants'. Too little tribute will cause a war or signal the decline of the nation it is owed to; having too few 'points' has the same effect on Paulie Walnuts—it plunges him into savagery and he 'goes forth with the weapons of his indignation' (in God's case, an earthquake or boils; in Paulie's, a gun or a baseball bat), and if satisfaction is denied him he declines into depression and superstition.

Like some of my own non-Sicilian ancestors, when Paulie's not being driven by his own indignation, he's trying to stir it in others. Rider Haggard wrote that Kipling once told him that this world had 'every attribute of hell: doubt, fear, pain, struggle, bereavement, almost irresistible temptations springing from the nature with which we are clothed, physical and mental suffering, etc., ending in the worst fate man can devise for man, Execution!' This is what Paulie wants the world to know—that everyone must suffer, what happens to him must happen to them. Paulie's boss, Tony Soprano, lives on the same precipice of despair. The show is a study in the relationship between indignation and depression. Christopher, Junior, Johnny Sack, Phil Leotardo—they are all two-year-olds. All manic depressives.

Long before, when we were children and could not even imagine families like the Sopranos, much less laugh at them, Steele Rudd's *On Our Selection* was the funniest thing in the house. The Rudd family were struggling Protestant selectors and before they were turned into buffoons for the screen, they were not far removed from small farming families like my own. It was the comedy, above all, that we recognised. The humour flowed from the meeting of Dad Rudd's noble nature and heroic intentions with intractable, inchoate and vindictive Nature: the droughts, the fires, the cockatoos and kangaroos, the feckless sons.

In one story, 'When the Wolf was at the Door', the family is penniless and has only pumpkin to eat. At the dinner table Dan asks Dave if he'd like some bread. 'Damn your insolence!' cries Dad, leaping to his feet.

'"Go!" said Dad, furiously, pointing to the door, "leave my roof, you thankless dog!"'

It is an Old Testament moment, and no doubt a Freudian one as well. In our illustrated edition, Dad was shown standing at the head of the table with the family sitting meekly round it. His beard was white, like God's, his eyes wild and he was pointing to the door. It was the one story that wasn't funny. The superego can never be funny of itself, only when it's punctured: as when, with the banished Dan still unsighted after many months, Dad grows testy again, and again in the manner of a Bible story—this time at the man's insufferable lack of gratitude. 'To leave me', he says, 'just when I wanted help! After all the years I've slaved to feed him and clothe him …!' It is both a laboured irony and an expression of the way indignation serves as a mainstay of the oldest human stories.

As the animal with the deepest sense of self, humans are the most likely to be offended. But they share the emotion with bonobos and chimpanzees, along with 99 per cent of their genes. Bonobos display all the primary emotions and high intelligence, kindness, empathy, even altruism. They can recognise themselves in mirrors. But in a film I saw about them, the most 'human' thing they did was get indignant.

A female (it is a matriarchal society) saw her child hurt by a playmate and punished the offender by breaking its finger—a life-threatening punishment for any animal that lives in the trees. The mother of the punished child in turn became indignant, and the ruckus made everyone else, including the males, as indignant as the two mothers. In the pandemonium that followed, the surrounding forest was torn half apart, and peace returned only after an all-in orgy from which no one—including the children—was excluded. The scene took place in the jungle of the Congo, but at least up to the orgy, it might have been in Canaan or Wagga.

The self includes children: in fact, in a healthy person, no insult will cause as much offence as an insult to her children. And nothing is surer to provoke me than an insult *from* a child.

These traits are found wherever dignity matters. I saw it one sunny day in the lions' enclosure at the Melbourne Zoo. The male lion slept in a dip beneath a grassy mound. On the slope above, a young lion rolled around, enjoying the sun and the freedom and the feel of his body. He stopped rolling for a moment and lay on his side, looking at the grown-up lion sleeping. It was like Ham looking on Noah. We could tell he knew the risk: but he did it anyway—he flopped over and rolled down the mound onto the lion, as if pretending it was an accident. The sleeping lion woke and leapt to his feet. For a moment he *was* Noah—or Dad Rudd. We expected a mighty roar and a mighty blow from his paw. But a look was all he gave the young lion, as if to say, 'Damn your insolence!' There is generally a moment when the indignant can retreat, when reason beckons dimly: but to follow it is like trying to turn back when your feet have left the diving board. It is against nature. This lion managed it just in time. He seemed to see the joke. It was just a kid, after all. His dignity was safe.

When she gave up being an actress, Grace Kelly became Her Serene Highness the Princess of Monaco, and the word 'Serene' would have done for the lion as he lay back down and closed his eyes. Serenity became him, as it should all kings—and queens, princes and princesses. Not for nothing are they sometimes called Serene or Most

Serene or Serenity. To be serene is to be clear, unclouded: to be above the clouds that befog the rest of us.

In *War and Peace* the Russian Field Marshal and Commander-in-Chief, Kutuzov, is 'flabby and swollen with fat', his face is savagely scarred from battle, one of his ears is stuffed with hemp and, though his horse is too small for him, he needs several Cossacks to help him off it. Kutuzov, however, is a prince—he became one after beating the French at Smolensk—and Tolstoy milks the irony of a man of his appearance and profession, in the midst of carnage and mayhem, answering to the honorific 'Serenity'. But in *War and Peace* that term finds a kind of literal expression in Kutuzov: and when the Field Marshal's decision to evacuate rather than defend Moscow leads to the destruction of Napoleon's army, Tolstoy gives Kutuzov's military calculation the power of an epiphany. Every Russian understood it, 'not on the basis of reasoning, but on the basis of the feeling that is inside us and was inside our fathers'. The decision, in other words, touches something in their souls that runs deeper than the normal expressions of patriotism: 'People nonchalantly awaited the enemy, did not riot, did not fret, did not tear anyone to pieces, but calmly awaited their fate ...' And when, by a seeming miracle, Russia is delivered, it is as if serenity has triumphed over indignation, a 'great man' has been thwarted by a modest one who saw what might be achieved by retreating from the usual patterns of aggression.

The example was set much earlier by the equanimity with which Socrates, Cato the Younger and Jesus faced death. Socrates took poison, Jesus died on the cross, and Cato, the legend goes, opened his own belly and took out his innards. They got their serenity—and their melancholy, which is the dark aspect of the same thing—from belief, from strength of mind. This is the hard way to do it. 'Cool' people do the same. By dress, patois, hairstyle, perfume—by cultivating a certain something—they escape the anxieties of the street. They make themselves as serene as majesties and highnesses.

Radicals imagine they see past that façade and, by puncturing their delusions, try to cause the toplofty as much offence as possible. 'If you tremble with indignation at every injustice then you are a comrade of mine', said Che Guevara, offering a prescription for perpetual agitation and torment. William James reasoned the same sentiment down to something an ordinary human being can live with:

> There is nothing to make one indignant in the mere fact that life is hard, that men should toil and suffer pain. But that so many men, by mere accidents of birth and opportunity, should have a life of nothing else but toil and pain and hardness and inferiority imposed upon them, should have *no* vacation, while others natively no more deserving never get any taste of this campaigning life at all—*this* is capable of raising indignation in reflective minds.

The American War of Independence owes a great deal to the European Enlightenment and to earlier writers, including Milton, who added a sense of high moral—if not Divine—purpose to the colonists' idea of liberty and the natural rights they imagined flowing from it. Of course it was not the philosophy *per se* that animated them, but the abundant self-esteem and moral certainty they derived from it. They had internalised the ideas, *become* the ideas: they made them, in Hermann Broch's words, 'to some extent a part of [their] personal biology'. Both—the colonists and the ideas—were sovereign: one and indivisible, we might say. Each spoke for the other; to offend one was to offend the other. If Britain offended against certain inalienable rights, embodying these rights as they believed they did, the colonists were insulted. They took them personally: had they taken them in the abstract, it might have been harder to leave slaves out of the equation.

The revolutionary ideology (or value-system) lives on: in the undying founding fathers and their equally undying rhetoric, in the unrelenting exegesis of the Constitution. Today, defaming any of these representations of the ideal, like defacing the flag, excites the same virtuous indignation that inflamed the revolutionaries. Those who do it in effect cross over to the enemy, and may expect contumely and ex-communication. The American republic is now an empire, but patriotism demands the republican rhetoric of its foundations, insisting in spite of much evidence to the contrary that those seminal ideas still guide the country. The extraordinary part is the extent to which they do. Barack Obama sought authority for change in the Constitution no less than Lincoln did. The phrases are still alive. Also alive is the original emotional impulse that turned those in possession of high ideas—and certain tangible interests—into revolutionaries.

The tone of American news media, the tribalism of the politicians, the flag-flying, the massive presence of the military, the gun fetish, the obsession with security, the fear and aggression, all speak of people easily insulted and easily incited. 'Just try it!' they say: 'How dare you even think it'.

Like mutant regressive Paul Reveres, the presenters of Fox News seem to believe it is their mission to keep the revolutionaries' rage alive and spluttering, to preserve the republic's first indignant moment in a 24/7 animated diorama. The windbags of television and radio are to modern society what the Queen of Hearts was to Lewis Carroll's imaginary one: caricatures of manic power, passing judgement much as horses pass wind and with as much resort to reason or proportion. But listen to them for half a day and the judgements reveal themselves as only surface eruptions, geysers spewing from a sea of resentment beneath the surface. The wonder is that so much indignation can be stored up in one radio announcer: but of course announcers draw their strength from all the underground streams of indignation across the land: from there and from the fabulous sums of money they are paid, and which they take to mean their opinions are indisputable if not divine. It doesn't matter that the listeners' demands are rarely if ever met: the Queen's demands for heads to roll never came to anything either. What matters is the general venting, the release of social steam, and the atmosphere of universal disgruntlement that the phenomenon unlocks. This creates the urgency, the imagined smell of sweat, aggression and stale rations and, above all, the *noise* of democracy on its original war footing.

In Australia the media climate is in general calmer, but a collective consciousness does gather round what is held to be self-evident common sense decorated with talismans that seem to shine brighter the further they drift from reality. 'The Fair Go', 'The Bush', Mateship and Anzac—let no one cast doubt on these 'values', or their personification in the late crocodile wrestler Steve Irwin.

The curious thing is that the complaints in general come from people who, if asked, would almost certainly insist that they live in the best country in the world, and indeed the best part of that country; and that democracy is far and away the best system. This only *seems* contradictory: in fact it is perfectly consistent with the view that every man and woman is as good as another, and this being so, they are all entitled to exercise arbitrary judgement about their fellow human beings and the world they live in—and what is more, in this advanced democracy, the technology is there for them to do it. You will hear them say on talkback or *Big Brother* that any opinion is as good as the next one, and no one has the right to 'disrespect my opinion'. My opinion might derive from Fantale wrappers. It might be incomprehensible or ridiculous. But my opinion is an expression of me, the sovereign me: me in my serene highness mode. 'I', if you don't mind. Of course indignation is the dominant emotion.

A culture of abundance creates abundant protest. In his reflection Narcissus saw someone he could fall in love with: in a narcissistic culture millions are disappointed every day. Our grandfathers cursed when they broke the handle of the shovel: we have several hundred items of convenience to fail us, betray their promise, reduce us. Many of our utilities are also fetishes, which is to say as much an investment in ourselves as in their utility. We make fetishes of everything, including our health and our children, and every time they fail or fluctuate we have an 'issue', which is a kind of fetishised difficulty. Issues must be resolved, by dialogue, doctors, consultants or lawyers. If they're not, we will be denied 'closure' (another fetish), and without closure we will not be able to 'move on' (yet another one). Our grandfathers moved on as soon as they had fixed the shovel.

William James detected 'ferocious pleasure' in anger, 'stern joy in the astringency and desolation'. In like vein, indignation (along with love and other higher emotions) had the seductive power to sweep away our 'inferior self': our inhibitions, cowardice, shyness, conventionality. It turns us into heroes, saints—monsters.

Thus Christ, who, according to the Gospel of St John, took to the moneychangers with 'a scourge of small cords'. As He is the Son of God, we are asked to believe that this was not indignation of the kind that grips us mortals; but rather, in the way of all divinely inspired conduct, it was somehow calculated, symbolic and the fulfilment of prophecy. It was anger without sin, righteous anger: anger of the kind that God expects of all believers when they encounter blasphemy or evil. Believe that if you like, but if Jesus had not taken out his righteous anger on the tables in the temple, and if he had not cursed the fig tree, the history of the world, including the very worst parts of the twentieth century, would have followed a different course, and one that could hardly be worse. If Jesus' indignation was calculated, it was not the kind of calculation most of us would own up to. But Satan might.

The British psychologist Donald Winnicott saw a direct connection between the art (and religion) of adult humans and the most inexplicable and alarming of all slights on our being, our weaning as infants. The symbols and rituals of adulthood, like the dolls and bears and bits of blanket (the 'transitional objects') carried everywhere by children, help us to live with that dreadful affront.

Like any state of excitement, to be indignant is to be not one's usual self; and being a state in which one's real or presumed self has been threatened, it is to feel an all but irresist-ible need to get on one's high horse and brain the offender at once. But writing and think-ing both take time and a rush of adrenaline is not always their friend. *Writing* indignantly is rather like slowly hitting someone with a brick, or slowly brushing a tarantula from one's cheek.

George Orwell was one of a rare species: a political creature with his sense of indigna-tion so well governed it actually helped his writing. 'When I sit down to write a book', he declared, 'I do not say to myself, "I am going to produce a work of art." I write it because there is some lie that I want to expose, some fact to which I want to draw attention, and my initial concern is to get a hearing.' His 'starting point', he said, was 'always a feeling of partisanship'. In most writers a wound to their political or moral sensibility is likely to inspire the 'purple passages, sentences without meaning, decorative adjectives and humbug generally' that Orwell deplored. But outrage had the opposite effect on Orwell. His best writing, he said, always had a political purpose; his worst 'invariably' lacked one.

In their social intercourse, people cultivate masks, blank stares and verbal blinds of various kinds to defend their dignity and hide the rush of blood provoked by insults. For much the same purpose offended writers put themselves at one remove by creating satires, burlesques and characters like Voltaire's Candide, Swift's Gulliver or Johnson's Rasselas: characters for whom naiveté serves as the mask and allows them to get to the bottom of human folly politely and without losing their reason.

Not everyone can do it. Compare the sinewy clarity of Orwell's prose—he aimed to make it like a 'window pane'—with the deep purple from Edmund Burke's philippic on British abuses of power in the eighteenth-century Raj: ' … the foul putrid mucus in which are engendered the whole brood of creeping ascarides, all the endless involutions, the eternal knot, added to a knot of those inexpugnable tape-worms which devour the nutriment and eat up the bowels of India …'

Burke was not always purple of course, and even when he was, the effect was often hair-raising. His 'inexpungable tape-worms', what's more, would do for, let's say, the Aboriginal experience of Northern Territory bureaucracy, and his 'endless involutions' for any number of privately owned public utilities that plague our lives. The entire passage may apply to any remote power, including some close to us, like banks or call centres, that at once provokes and stifles indignation and in this way leaves us feeling less than human.

It was lucky for everyone that Burke's verbal resources ran as deep as his feelings. Such a phenomenon of sustained outrage as his years-long pursuit of Warren Hastings and the East India Company required equally phenomenal metaphors rendered in language of boundless variety—or else be brushed off as the ranting of a maniac or an Irishman. Burke once said that Hastings could not dine 'without creating a famine', and his life would have been well worth living if that had been the only thing he ever said. While it is probably true to say that his savaging of Hastings aroused just enough sympathy for the man to get him acquitted, it also helped establish some new moral principles for colonial governance: new because until then, presumably, Englishmen had not thought Indians sufficiently human for the inhuman abuse of them to be worth getting indignant about.

'Indignation devours me ...', Flaubert said. He wanted to 'purge' himself of it. The feeling consumed the last decades of his life. The bourgeoisie, the working classes, the peasantry, the intellectuals—every social category offended him. *Democracy* offended him. Mankind in its 'irremediable wretchedness', in particular as it presented itself in the 1870 Paris Commune, offended him. Above all, stupidity offended him, and nearly everyone was stupid. 'I can no longer talk with anyone at all without becoming furious, and everything I read by my contemporaries makes me quiver with indignation', he wrote to Turgenev. The only thing he was not indignant about was his own youthful behaviour, which, to be charitable, was nearly as stupid as anything he encountered in his mature years. And his intolerance of stupidity almost certainly had roots in his dire awareness of our inability to know very much about anything. The two idiots of his unfinished novel, *Bouvard and Pécuchet*, read an entire library and know infinitely less at the end than the nothing they knew when they set out. So with Flaubert: the more he learned the more he came to see that 'We still know almost nothing and we would wish to divine the final word that will never be revealed to us'. The stupid touched something very personal in Flaubert—namely knowledge of his own ignorance. The stupid came blindly trampling over the terrible secret. 'O God, thou knowest my foolishness.'

Even if it can't be said with certainty of Flaubert, it seems likely that the degree of our indignation is related to the degree of our guilt. To choose a topical example: if some decent people get indignant about pictures of naked children in modern works of art while others just as decent don't, is that because the second group are less decent in the matter of children, or because the first group are? Are the second lot simply insensible to the moral danger the first lot see, or are the first lot compensating for disturbing feelings the pictures stir in them?

I would number myself among those people who don't feel much offended by Bill Henson's photographs while conceding that they are not in every case morally vigilant or as strict with themselves as they should be. They do not feel themselves threatened by pictures of naked children, they do not feel their children are threatened by them and, perhaps because a bit of nakedness really never hurt anybody, they do not feel the child in the photograph is threatened. It might be for these reasons that the matter does not spark their indignation; it might be because they feel indignant about too much else, or because stupidity or cultural theory has left them without the capacity to feel indignant about anything; or it might be that they have an aversion to particular kinds of moral indignation—especially the kind which cannot co-exist with ambiguity, a sense of humour, or any other sense that might grant us tolerance and self-awareness. There is always a sense with the morally indignant that their real aim is to console themselves.

'The voice of honest indignation is the voice of God', William Blake said. And that, on occasion, is the trouble with it. The morally indignant speak as if on His behalf. There is the righteous indignation of an Edmund Burke or an Emmeline Pankhurst or a Martin Luther King, and there is the righteous indignation of people who confuse virtue with loathing vice and seeing it behind every door and shrub. There is the indignation of Jonathan Swift and the indignation of Barnaby Joyce. There is Alexander Solzhenitsyn's indignation and there is Jack Benny's schtick. One would think, given the extremes of human experience, God might have granted us some more specific mechanisms for dealing with it. There is indignation over the unnecessary suffering of millions, and indignation over a bad haircut. The related worlds of television, talkback radio and social media swarm with the indignant. There is the indignation of the victims and the indignation of the powerful and entitled who reckon resistance is a denial of their natural rights. There is indignation of the kind necessary to resist tyranny and exploitation, whether they are practised by a petty bureaucrat or a dictator, and there is the indignation used to justify them. There is real, feigned and imagined indignation. It is one of life's great conjuring acts for any human being to settle on the right kind in the right proportion.

Indignation might be viewed as the psychological equivalent of the body's immune system, which, when it recognises a virus threatening our equilibrium or existence, manufactures quantities of phlegm and mucus to protect us. Very often we speak as if the effects were the same when a slight invades us and we lack the eloquence to discharge our wounded feelings: we gag on them, become speechless: 'Here he got choked by excessive indignation ...' Conrad says of one of his characters in *Heart of Darkness*. Winston Churchill recognised the syndrome when he called across the House to a noisy political opponent: 'The honourable gentleman should not really generate more indignation than he can contain.' In the same chamber in 1939, as Chamberlain propounded his egregious position on German territorial demands, an honourable member was reported to have thrown up, which seems to confirm Darwin's observation: 'Extreme disgust is expressed by movements around the mouth identical with those preparatory to the act of vomiting.'

In general, the immune system gets it right, but there are times when it protests too much and becomes more virulent—and more deadly—than the invading virus. It is called a cytokine storm and most of us have seen parallel symptoms in the aggrieved: outbursts out of all proportion to the offence, capable of causing lethal strokes and heart attacks in the offended and painful if not actually dangerous to bystanders.

Like the souls it seeks to defend, indignation is sometimes an ennobling spectacle and an agent of welcome progress, and just as often ugly and destructive. It is the natural stuff of politics, just as it is of gangster films: stuff with which to bolster oneself, reduce others and manipulate as many as possible. No one can master politics if she has not mastered indignation—her own, her supporters' and her opponents'.

Hitler's revolution, like those of other ideological stripes, was substantially built on indignation; and like the others, once established, maintained itself by projecting onto the minds of citizens myriad counter-revolutionary phantoms, subversive elements, enemies of the people, treasonous tendencies and so on—each of them not only a threat to stable government, but an affront to the ambitions and sacrifices of the people and their glorious leaders. In both Hitler's Germany and Stalin's Russia the language of indignation was used to *eradicate* feelings of indignation. The effect of this—combined of course with the threat of exile, torture and execution—was to create at worst surly complicity, but more often a collective raising of hackles. Indignation is not only contagious; it is also addictive, as most people who have lived in a family or played contact sports will know. After a while we need the adrenaline: it feels better than thinking, which might be why all societies seem to need some level of hysteria pretty well all the time.

If to be indignant is to stand on one's dignity, totalitarianism makes sure that nobody can. Anyone who has felt the invisible, 'hypnotic force' invade him and 'dissolve his will', Vasily Grossman wrote, will be 'astonished that a man can rebel against it even for a moment'. Possibly it was because the Soviet regime had crushed their dignity that the bulk of the Russian population could not muster much resistance when a band of the old oppressors filched their country's wealth; and why when a kleptocrat and thug came forth echoing both Stalin and the Tsars, they cheered. As if to restore their lost dignity he spoke of 'Great Russia', and constructed a unique Russian world view out of largely imagined 'Russianness'. Restoring their pride and identity enlarged their capacity for taking offence, and his for manipulating them.

Hitler's genius—and we only call it this because he had so much time to practise—was to keep his propaganda personal and concrete. Every good speechwriter knows this is the only way to do it: find some poor cove with a story of misfortune or modest triumph to tell, and run your admiration or your indignation through him. Make him your Stakhanov, your message made flesh. Among democratic politicians Bill Clinton made an art of it, and Eleanor Roosevelt came gently to the conclusion that her 'interest or sympathy or indignation is not aroused by an abstract cause but by the plight of a single person whom I have seen with my own eyes. Out of my response to an individual develops an awareness of a problem to the community, then to the country and finally to the world'. Hitler came to the same conclusion. He began with himself, and eventually had millions of other 'single persons' at his disposal. He got them in the main by making sure their enemies were no more abstract than they were. The Jews, the Bolsheviks, the traitors of Versailles, the homosexuals, the unfit: all those for whom he felt visceral fear and hatred he moved his followers to fear and hate. Because all of them were threats to German dignity, all good Germans were perforce indignant.

No doubt neuroscience could tell us what part of the brain is excited by an insult: the amygdala that fear lights up, or the anterior insula that is activated by pain—physical *and* emotional, we are told. Whatever the neuro-logical case, the response is reactive rather than deliberative. It is also very likely addic-tive, in the way that fear and pain can be. The Hitlers of the world, along with religious zealots and modern populists and dema-gogues, work with chemicals. They also work in mythic realms, wherein we find much of our identity and self-worth, and therefore our capacity for offence. 'Make America Great Again', used by both Trump and Reagan, is a mythic slogan. Think not only of those two, but of FDR and Bob Hawke: even when they have a considerable capacity for reason-ing, effective politicians are also very good at manipulating myth. Neuroscience might yet prove that this is also a matter of chemicals. Populist politicians deal in the most basic and volatile elements of the human personality, and the skilful (or really mad) ones find enough to animate mobs and nations.

When George W Bush supercharged the outrage after 9/11 with belligerence and lies and rode the wave of dudgeon into Iraq, he added his name to the numberless leaders of petty tribes and great empires who have roused their followers to war with similar concoctions. The United States was born in indignation, and its cruder politicians ever since have sought the same emotional terrain for exploitation. Lincoln personified the other kind, the kind who wrote the founding documents to douse unreason: the reason-seeking, deliberative kind: 'Let us do nothing through passion and ill temper. Even though the Southern people will not so much as listen to us, let us calmly consider their demands …', he told his Republican audience in the speech that made him at Cooper Union in 1860. He soon found that the Southern people were addicted to their indignation, and could no more give it up than they could their corn liquor, or their slaves.

Following Lincoln's example and determined not to present as an angry black man, Barack Obama sought conciliation with his opponents, only to find as Lincoln did that his opponents were implacable enemies. Obama never looked like an angry black man: instead he looked like a super cool one, which was almost as provocative. If in the early days of his Presidency he had spoken unequivocally for the victims of the 2008 financial disaster and pursued half a dozen of those responsible to gaol, had he roused the country's righteous fury to his side, the course and tenor of American politics must have been very different—and Donald Trump, who with Bernie Sanders swept up *all* the simmering rage, might not be President.

But the uncool have spoken and Donald Trump *is* President. Like George W Bush going to Iraq, Trump was rolled into the White House by a hybrid mob united by their sense that they—sovereign citizens of the greatest nation the world has ever known—were being taken for granted. How dare they! The Washington elites, the Clintons, the Obamas, the Chinese, the Democrats, the Republicans, the Mexicans, immigrants in general; the liberals, the politically correct, the uppity blacks, the uppity women, blacks and women in general: whoever 'they' were, their time was up. It hardly matters if the grievances had roots in reality or fakery or stupidity or envy or fear or imagination or evangelism, when they were offered a choice between indignation and what with good reason they took for complacency and entitlement they chose to be indignant. The sovereign citizens of the greatest nation said let's make this malign nitwit our President and to hell with the consequences. No doubt there were Democrats who wondered later if in the wrathful climate the other indignant candidate, Sanders, might have been more successful than the smug embodiment of the neoliberal status quo they chose.

Nothing animates a nation and unleashes force like indignation. With Iraq, George W

Bush was following an example so ancient and reliable we might as well concede that the trait in human beings is irremediable. Contrive a brazen outrage and identify the culprit, and the drums begin to beat. The 'half dozen rash spirits' (as Mark Twain called them) who are generally there to resist the rush to war might offer more original and mature thought, but not much practical salvation.

Donald Trump is contemptible and leaves decency aghast; yet for offence George W Bush surpasses him. There he was, the world's most powerful person, behaving as if he was at best a cipher for more powerful people around him, at worst a brat who stole the throne—worse still, had it stolen for him. That might be tolerable if he had been capable of imitating a real President: Lincoln or Roosevelt would be asking too much, but even Reagan and Carter were beyond his talents. We all of us have an idea of leadership which is offended by the pretence of it in someone as inadequate as Dubya. It's a kind of blasphemy. It insults our inner Abraham. When Bush's speechwriters feebly imitated the cadences of Lincoln and the King James Version, but offered no trace of the thought that drives them, it was an insult. When he wore a military uniform, though Grant and Eisenhower, real soldiers, never wore a uniform as President, it was an insult. When he talked in that homespun way as if he had come down from Mark Twain, but gave no other sign that he had ever read a word of him or had a fibre in common with him, it was an insult. When he not only lacked wisdom but seemed to glory in his ignorance; when he and others in the cabal spoke of Munich and appeasement, as if his opponents were Chamberlains and they all Churchills, as if they had a halfway credible grasp of history, it was an insult.

When, unlike any of these real leaders, he had done nothing and read nothing from which he might have learned something; when he seemed indifferent to cruelty, unconcerned by his failures and unable to escape the emotional void outrageous privilege had bestowed on him, it was beyond sufferance. And when he insisted that he was heir to the Judeo-Christian tradition and took advice from the God of the Old Testament (whom he called the 'Higher Father'); as if he had lived so much as a week by the sweat of his brow and as if his life was anything more than evidence for those who say the Higher Father either never was or is no more—that was pure blasphemy. It was not the religion in George W Bush but the absence of it that this atheist could not stand. And that he will never be punished for this sham, or for the never-ending nightmare his hubris and stupidity—his indulgent indignation—inflicted, makes the insult an undying one.

I did not ask for George W Bush. I did not vote for him. He was imposed on me, and his every hollow word and gesture was that much more noxious and invasive for being bloated with presumption. How dare this foreign idiot have a platform in my living room, my Prime Minister welcome him, lap up his compliments, grovel like a spaniel in his company.

Bush became an extension of my being, like a tumour, a neurosis or a flea. In a dream I took him for a ride in my car, past my old primary school that is no longer there, past the old cypresses that are no longer there. I offered him friendship, tried to draw him out of himself. But he just sat there in the back seat, never looking at the sights. Is there anything more galling than an insouciant guest? I could see him in the mirror, slouching there with that vacant expression of the half-daft princeling that he is. I was polite, but seethed with the biblical desire to pulverise him. The truth is we would not have had him to the kitchen—not when he walked like that, and slumped in his chair and dropped his 'g's.

Indignation is such a tiring emotion. It excites the mind and impoverishes it at the same time. It is *never* reasonable. Yet everything moves this way. A serene Achilles neither retires from the battle nor returns to it, and Homer's left without a hero. Gods who are not indignant may as well be lumps of stone—or melancholy. Symbols not of human possibility but of defeat. It is the same with us, naturally.

In Northamptonshire, fifteen years ago, I met an Englishman who had served in the Royal Engineers in both World Wars: on the Somme and at Normandy. The Somme was not so bad, he said. I thought this odd. Thereafter the conversation went something like this:

'Didn't you ever get depressed?' I had to shout because he was 106 and very deaf.

'When?' he shouted back.

'In the trenches with the shells exploding, and all that death, and losing your mates!'

'Why would I?' he said, as if the very thought were poisonous.

I was wondering if 106 years hadn't ground away his faculties, when he yelled to his carer to bring his tea.

'There's a piece of cheddar, three crackers and a pickled onion. And where's Puss?'

'Outside', said the carer.

'What!' shouted the veteran. 'Outside! On a night like this! Never put the cat outside—never ever without asking me. Do you hear me!'

'So you quite enjoyed the war?'

'Of course! Why wouldn't I? I was glad to do my duty. People your age don't understand duty. Is the onion there? Where's Puss? I'll put YOU outside and see how you like it!'

Read
'On'

Little Books
on
Big Themes

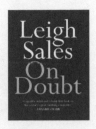

'A superbly stylish and valuable
little book on this century's great
vanishing commodity.'
Annabel Crabb

Acclaimed journalist Leigh Sales has her doubts, and
thinks you should, too. Her classic personal essay
carries a message about the value of truth, scrutiny and
accountability—a much-needed, pocket-sized antidote
to fake news.

Donald Trump, the post-truth world and the instability
of Australian politics are all examined in this fresh take
on her prescient essay on the media and political trends
that define our times.

mup.com.au

'A delicate confession of the implications of lust and
longing on a girl's sexual awakening ...'
Marta Dusseldorp

On Lust and *On Longing* together for the first time.

When *On Lust* was first published it caused a media
sensation: Blanche d'Alpuget wrote of a pillar of society
who had molested children and of events that ended in
mystery. Now she reveals all. *On Longing* caused a similar
sensation, for different reasons. D'Alpuget dared to write
that she loved and had inspired love in a man already
adored by the public.

Here are the raw and timeless themes of the power and
powerlessness inherent to lust, love, loss and death.

mup.com.au

'This is the book we all need right now. Gemmell
nails how to achieve serenity and calm amid all the
crazy busyness of modern living.'
Lisa Wilkinson

International bestselling author Nikki Gemmell
writes on the power of quiet in today's shouty world.

Quiet comes as a shock in these troubled times.

Quietism means 'devotional contemplation and
abandonment of the will … a calm acceptance of things
as they are'. Gemmell makes the case for why quiet is
steadily gaining ground in this noisy age: Why we need
it now more than ever. How to glean quiet, hold on to it,
and work within it.

mup.com.au

'A crisp, forceful call to reflect on the meaning
of disruption; Murphy places her stethoscope
firmly on the chest of the modern media, calls it
to account and reveals an uncertain, uncomfortable,
but enduring heartbeat.'
Julia Baird

The internet has shaken the foundations of life: public and
private lives are wrought by the 24-hour, seven-day-a-week
news cycle that means no one is ever off duty.

On Disruption is a report from the coalface of that change:
what has happened, will it keep happening,
and is there any way out of the chaos?

mup.com.au

Sarah Ferguson
On Mother

'An elegantly written, deeply personal story
of a daughter's grief after her mother's sudden
and mysterious death, with a true-crime
investigation at its heart.'
Jennifer Byrne

A mother's love over decades and across continents.
The sudden death of Sarah's mother reveals their
relationship with poignant clarity and shows her the
individual who existed beyond motherhood. A reflection
on mothers and daughters.

'A great bedtime read on the epidemic of
sleep deprivation and insomnia pervading
our modern work lives.'
Sabra Lane

On Sleep is the story of our love–hate relationship
with slumber.

Part-time insomniac Fleur Anderson ponders the big
questions: Why can't I sleep? Do politicians and other
high-fliers ever admit they too are exhausted? Do they get
enough sleep to make sensible decisions? Where is society
heading, and why did I have that glass of cab sav?